A Little Book of
Happiness

A Little Book of
Happiness

Ruskin Bond

SPEAKING
TIGER

SPEAKING TIGER PUBLISHING PVT. LTD
4381/4 Ansari Road, Daryaganj,
New Delhi–110002, India

Anthology copyright © Speaking Tiger 2016
Introduction copyright © Ruskin Bond 2016

ISBN: 978-93-85755-94-1
eISBN: 978-93-85755-98-9

10 9 8 7 6 5 4 3

Typeset in Garamond Pro by SÜRYA, New Delhi
Printed at Thomson Press, Delhi

All rights reserved.
No part of this publication may be reproduced,
transmitted, or stored in a retrieval system,
in any form or by any means, electronic,
mechanical, photocopying, recording
or otherwise, without the prior
permission of the publisher.

This book is sold subject to the condition that it
shall not, by way of trade or otherwise, be lent,
resold, hired out, or otherwise circulated,
without the publisher's prior consent,
in any form of binding or cover other
than that in which it is published.

Introduction

Last Saturday, when I was autographing books at the local bookshop, a young college student asked me, 'What is the secret of happiness?'

At first I couldn't think of an answer, except to say, 'It's no secret. Happiness is right next to you'—with particular reference to the pretty girl who accompanied him.

But thinking about it now, I suppose happiness means different things to different people.

Beena is happiest in her pooja room, or when she is on the phone talking to her children—Siddharth in New Delhi, Shrishti in Bhubaneshwar, Gautam in Dehradun.

Rakesh is happy behind the wheel of his car; the last place where I would be happy, having once driven through a garden wall in Friends Colony, New Delhi.

Nor am I happy on a motor-cycle, which is where Siddharth likes to be happy. And you won't find me in the Beauty Parlour, frequented by Shrishti when she's home on holiday.

Some people are miserable when it's raining heavily and they can't go shopping. I'm quite happy on a rainy day because then I can curl up on a sofa, visit Blandings Castle with P.G. Wodehouse, enjoy a village cricket match with Mr Pickwick and his Dickensian friends, or go rowing on the Thames with Jerome K. Jerome's three men and a dog. A good book on a rainy day is happiness for me.

As a writer I am also happy when I have completed a story or poem or essay and feel pleased with it. On the other hand, failed creations make me unhappy and I don't like leaving anything unfinished. If I am not happy with something I have written, it goes into the waste-paper basket.

We all have to do something in life, and if our occupation or vocation or profession gives us pleasure, well, that's happiness.

So choose well, my friend. Before you launch out on the journey of life, make sure that the career or lifestyle that you have chosen is something that you really want to follow.

And may some of the words in this little book help you to realize your dreams.

Ruskin Bond
April, 2016

To find happiness, look halfway between too little and too much.

> 'Happiness is as good as food.'
> —*An African proverb*

❧

> 'One joy scatters a hundred griefs.'
> —*Anonymous*

❧

Having bumbled through eighty years without permanent injury, I am no wiser than an old cabbage! I only know that for the most part I have followed instinct rather than intelligence, and this has resulted in a modicum of happiness. Life hasn't been a bed of roses. And yet, quite often, I've had roses out of season.

Happiness is not waiting to be found; there's no use looking for it. All we need to do is to find the barriers within ourselves that we have built against it. Trust—in people, in life—is a good way to begin.

'Why not seize the pleasure at once? How often is happiness destroyed by preparation, foolish preparation!'
—*Jane Austen*

I come upon my friend Pitamber
dancing on the road one night.
'Why are you dancing in the
middle of the road?' I ask.
'Because I am happy,' he says.
'And why are you so happy?'
He looks at me as if I am a fool.
'Because I am dancing in the
middle of the road,' he says.

Feeling down and out? Lift up your head and shout—'It's a great day!'

❧

Happiness is a matter of temperament rather than circumstance. To take life lightly and in good humour is to get the most out of it.

❧

.Ruskin Bond.

Whether by accident or design,
we are here.
Let's make the most of it,
my friend.
Make happiness our pursuit,
Spread a little sunshine
here and there.
Enjoy the flowers, the breeze,
Rivers, sea and sky,
Mountains and tall waving trees.
Greet the children passing by,
Talk to the old folk,
be kind, my friend.
Hold on in times of pain
and strife;
Until death comes, all is life.

Happiness is as elusive as a
butterfly, and we must never
pursue it. If we stay very still,
it may come and settle on our
hand. But only briefly. We must
learn to savour the moment.

'We must be willing to let go of
the life we have planned,
so as to have the life that is
waiting for us.'
—*E.M. Forster*

Notes

_____
_____
_____
_____
_____
_____
_____
_____
_____
_____
_____

.Ruskin Bond.

.20.

.Ruskin Bond.

Happy is he whose heart sees more clearly than his eyes.

Expect good, and good will come.

To be happy, you must have compassion—not only for the world, but also for yourself. And you should know that contentment is easier to attain than happiness, and that it is enough.

For all its hardships and complications, life is simple, and a nature that doesn't sue for happiness often receives it in large measure.

❧

'That man is happiest who lives from day to day and asks no more, garnering the simple goodness of life.'
—*Euripides*

❧

'Be happy. It's one way of
being wise.'
—*Colette*

'To be without some of
the things you want is an
indispensable part of happiness.'
—*Bertrand Russell*

The first condition of happiness
is that a man must find joy
in his work.

I have yet to meet a neurotic
carpenter or stonemason or
clay-worker or master craftsman
of any kind. Those who fashion
beautiful things with their hands
are usually well-balanced people.

The fewer your desires, the
greater your happiness.

❧

'If a straw can tickle a man, it is
an instrument of happiness.'
—*John Dryden*

❧

There is no happiness without love. And to find love you don't go looking for it; you only need to open the doors and windows to your heart. And if the love does not last, there will be memories to keep you warm on cold and gloomy days.

The wind carries the muted sound of conversation, the hillside rings with laughter. There's a celebration somewhere. From a distance, these are good sounds on a cold and silent night. The thought of happy people in the neighbourhood puts me in a good mood.

.30.

.Ruskin Bond.

.31.

.Ruskin Bond.

If more of us valued
food and cheer
and song above
hoarded gold,
it would be a merrier world.

— J.R.R. Tolkien

Into the woods on an October afternoon. I lie in the sun, on sweet-smelling grass, and gaze up through a pattern of oak leaves into a blinding blue heaven. And I praise god for leaves and grass and the smell of things—the smell of mint and bruised clover—and the touch of things—the touch of grass and air and the sky's blueness.

.Ruskin Bond.

This morning I was pondering on the absence of a philosophy or religious outlook in my make-up, and feeling a little low because it was cloudy and dark outside. Then the clouds broke up and the sun came out and almost immediately I felt an uplift of spirit. No philosophy would be of use to a person so susceptible to changes in light and shade. No philosophy would be necessary.

'The happiness of your life
depends upon the quality of
your thoughts.'
—*Marcus Aurelius*

'If you don't have horns you are
not a bull, and if you are not
warm and friendly you
can't be happy.'
—*A Bhutanese proverb*

'All suffering there is in the world
comes from desiring only myself
to be happy.'
—*Shantideva*

'Some day you will find out that
there is far more happiness in
another's happiness than
in your own.'
—*Honoré de Balzac*

Grow a garden, or some leaves and flowers in old tin cans or plastic buckets. Water each plant every morning, giving it your full attention. Stand back and watch the water sparkling on leaf and petal, and you are ready to face the stormiest of days.

Ruskin Bond.

Among the Turks there is
a saying: Patience attracts
happiness; it brings near
that which is far.

❧

And among the Masais there is
this belief: Happy is he whose
own faults prevent him from
castigating the faults of others.

❧

If we have never been unhappy,
how will we know when
happiness comes?

❧

Two things make life worth
living: a good joke and a good
digestion.

❧

.Ruskin Bond.

.43.

.A Little Book of Happiness.

Winter sunshine,
a child's laughter,
the smell of frying onions,
a kiss in the dark,
the first monsoon shower—
these simple things contribute
more to our happiness than
acts of passion and excitement.

Contemplating the tiny ladybird on the wild rose gives one hope that there is more to life than interest rates, dividends, market forces and infinite technology. There is space for the big and the small; there is space for you and me and the ladybird.

.Ruskin Bond.

'When the first baby laughed for the first time, the laugh broke into a thousand pieces and they all went skipping about, and that was the beginning of fairies.'
—*J.M. Barrie*

'Don't let one cloud obliterate the whole sky.'
—*Anaïs Nin*

If I am fit enough to gambol, I must gambol. Why should it matter that I am old? The world is like a cheerless headmaster, always telling you to behave. It likes to put you in a box, but you must never let it succeed. The inside of a box is not a happy place.

❧

.Ruskin Bond.

I may not have contributed
anything towards the progress
of civilization, but neither have
I robbed the world of anything.
Even the spider on the wall is
welcome to his space. After all,
he gives me mine, and we
are both at peace.

'Happiness is when what you think, what you say and what you do are in harmony.'
—*Mahatma Gandhi*

'Happiness is the only good, reason the only torch, justice the only worship, humanity the only religion and love the only priest.'
—*Robert G. Ingersoll*

'Those born to wealth, and who
have the means of gratifying
every wish, know not what is the
real happiness of life,
just as those who have been
tossed on the stormy waters of
the ocean on a few frail planks
can alone realize the blessings
of fair weather.'
—*Alexandre Dumas*

'Life works upon a compensating balance, and the happiness we gain in one direction we lose in another. As our means increase, so do our desires; and we ever stand midway between the two. When we reside in an attic, we enjoy a supper of fried fish and stout. When we occupy the first floor, it takes an elaborate dinner at the Continental to give us the same amount of satisfaction.'

—*Jerome K. Jerome*

Notes

_____
_____
_____
_____
_____
_____
_____
_____
_____
_____
_____
_____

.55.

.56.

There is no happiness like that of being loved by your fellow creatures, and feeling that your presence is an addition to their comfort.

— Charlotte Brontë

A local racketeer, who has been
in jail a couple of times, meets
me on the road and compliments
me because I'm 'always smiling'.
I think better of him for
the observation.

If you can smile when you feel
hurt, the hurt is half cured.

Happiness is not the opposite of sorrow. They co-exist; in that acceptance we take the first step towards inner peace.

'Happiness always lingers with unhappiness. They are two sides of the same coin. When the whole coin drops from your hand you are neither happy nor unhappy.'
—*Osho*

'Don't cry because it's over, smile because it happened.'
—*Dr Seuss*

❧

We have as much right to cry as we have to laugh. Men given to tears are good men, goes an old Greek saying.

❧

If a tortoise could run,
And losses be won,
And bullies be buttered on toast;
If a song brought a shower,
And a gun grew a flower,
This world would be better
than most.

'I felt my lungs inflate with
the onrush of scenery—air,
mountains, trees, people.
I thought, "This is what it
is to be happy."'
—*Sylvia Plath*

One of life's greatest pleasures is
free. It lies in watching a plant
grow—from seed to seedling, to
green branch to bough,
to flower to fruit.

'Having a great intellect is no
path to being happy.'
—*Stephen Fry*

'Laughter is the language of
the soul.'
—*Pablo Neruda*

Live close to nature and your
spirit will not be easily broken,
for you learn something of
patience and resilience. You will
not grow restless, and you will
never feel lonely.

A mynah bird alights on the
window sill, delivers a short
speech, waits for me to nod
my approval and takes off. My
birthday gift in advance.

Notes

.Ruskin Bond.

If you want happiness for an hour — take a nap.

— A Chinese proverb

Last night, as I lay sleepless
In the summer dark
With window open to invite
a breeze,
Softly a firefly flew in
And circled round the room
Twinkling at me from floor
or ceiling,
Lighting up little spaces—
A friendly presence, dispelling
The settled gloom of an
unhappy day.

❧

.Ruskin Bond.

'Never despair.'
—*Horace*

❧

Never believe those who tell you that there are no second beginnings in life. Every day is a chance to start afresh. Very often, all satisfaction and achievement is in the effort.

❧

The whistling thrush is here, bathing in the rainwater puddle beneath my window. His blue-black wings glitter in the sunshine. He loves this spot. So now, when there is no rain, I fill the puddle with water, just so my favourite bird keeps coming.

'For every minute you are angry
you lose sixty seconds
of happiness.'
—*Ralph Waldo Emerson*

Three mantras of happiness:

Think of old friends.
Make new friends.
Become your own best friend.

'A sure way to lose happiness, I've found, is to want it at the expense of everything else.'
—*Bette Davis*

'Do not anticipate trouble, or worry about what may never happen. Keep in the sunlight.'
—*Benjamin Franklin*

'If you want to be happy, be.'
—*Leo Tolstoy*

Happiness does not arrive with fireworks. It settles in quietly, long before you recognize it. And sometimes it is gone before you do.

'People who dream when they sleep at night know of a special kind of happiness which the world of the day holds not, a placid ecstasy and ease of heart that are like honey on the tongue. They also know that the real glory of dreams lies in their atmosphere of unlimited freedom.'
—*Karen Blixen*

_____
_____
_____
_____
_____
_____
_____
_____
_____
_____
_____

.Ruskin Bond.

You will never be happy
if you continue to search
for what happiness consists of.
You will never live if you
are looking for the meaning of life

If we have the eyes to see, and ears to listen, the world is never without things to soothe the heart. Each day there is birdsong and moonlight, flowers and old familiars, food to satisfy our hunger and water to quench our thirst.

.Ruskin Bond.

I like a sausage, I do;
It's a dish for the chosen and few.
Oh, for a sausage and mash,
And of mustard a dash,
And an egg nicely fried—
maybe two?

> 'Learn to let go. That is the key to happiness.'
> —*A Buddhist teaching*

> 'It is more fitting for a man to laugh at life than to lament over it.'
> —*Seneca*

'There is only one way to happiness and that is to cease worrying about things which are beyond the power of our will.'
—*Epictetus*

'Happiness is a gift and the trick is not to expect it, but to delight in it when it comes.'
—*Charles Dickens*

'When we are happy, we are always good, but when we are good, we are not always happy.'
—*Oscar Wilde*

A life of constant virtue, like a life of constant vice, can only end in misery.

Don't be depressed by your surroundings. That pebble at your feet has as much beauty as any great work of art.

❧

I don't have to climb the Eiffel Tower to see a city spread out before me. Every night I see the lights of the Doon twinkling in the valley below; each night is a festive occasion.

❧

Some people choose to sail around the world in small boats. Others remain in their own small patch, yet see the world in a grain of sand.

'Happiness is not a horse, you cannot harness it.'
—*A Russian proverb*

_____
_____
_____
_____
_____
_____
_____
_____
_____
_____
_____
_____

.90.

.Ruskin Bond.

With mirth and laughter
let old wrinkles
come.

— William Shakespeare

Listen to the night wind
in the trees,
Listen to the summer
grass singing;
Listen to the time that's
tripping by,
And the dawn dew falling.
Listen to the moon as it
climbs the sky,
Listen to the pebbles humming;
Listen to the mist in the
trembling leaves,
And the silence calling.

.Ruskin Bond.

'Happiness is never grand.'
—*Aldous Huxley*

'The true secret of happiness lies in taking a genuine interest in all the details of daily life.'
—*William Morris*

'God bless the inventor of sleep,
the cloak that covers all
men's thoughts.'
—*Cervantes*

A pillow can make all the difference to one's life. Sleep with the wrong pillow and you'll wake up an angry man. The right pillow, and you wake up a happy man.

And here's a gem from a book of Bhutanese wisdom: 'Do not chirrup too much about your happiness, and do not whine too much about your unhappiness.'

Which makes me think: happiness shared is an act of compassion; happiness flaunted, an act of violence.

'I shall take the heart. For brains do not make one happy, and happiness is the best thing in the world.'
—*L. Frank Baum*

'We all look for happiness, but without knowing where to find it: like drunkards who look for their house, knowing dimly that they have one.'
—*Voltaire*

Love is as mysterious as
happiness—no telling when it
may visit us; when it will look in
at the door and walk on, or come
in and decide to stay.
May both love and happiness
enter your life, dear reader,
and decide to stay.

For most people loneliness is
wrongly linked to unhappiness.
Their minds are not deep enough
to appreciate the sweetness
and balm of solitude.

'Of all the means to insure
happiness throughout the
whole of life,
by far the most important is the
acquisition of friends.'
—*Epicurus*

.A Little Book of Happiness.

.Ruskin Bond.

A moment of happiness, you and I sitting on a verandah, apparently two, but one in soul, you and I

— Rumi

As in life, so in art: only connect. I have always believed that to communicate and be readable is all that a writer should aim for. For a writer—as for any artist, whether a painter or a comedian—there can be no greater joy than this connection.

'The crowning fortune of a man is to be born to some pursuit which finds him employment and happiness, whether it be to make baskets, or broadswords, or canals, or statues, or songs.'
—*Ralph Waldo Emerson*

❧

How many dreams might have become happy realities but for that terrible sentence, 'Too much trouble!'

❧

'One swallow does not make a summer, neither does one fine day. Similarly, one day or a brief time of happiness does not make a person entirely happy.'

Thus spoke Aristotle. But brief times of happiness can be sufficient gifts for a lifetime. No one is entirely happy for all time.

🌿

'Happiness when you are miserable:
To plant Japanese poppies with cornflowers and mignonette, and bed out the petunias among the sweet-peas so that they shall perfume each other. To see sweet-peas coming up.
To drink very good tea out of a thin Worcester cup
of a colour between apricot and pink shell…'
—*Rumer Godden*

'I, not events, have the power to make me happy or unhappy today. I can choose which it shall be. Yesterday is dead, tomorrow hasn't arrived yet. I have just one day, today, and I'm going to be happy in it.'
—*Groucho Marx*

'All of man's miseries stem from his inability to sit quietly in a room alone.'
—*Blaise Pascal*

'Why should we build our happiness on the opinions of others, when we can find it in our own hearts?'
—*Jean-Jacques Rousseau*

To be able to laugh and to be able to care—just this much will ensure a good life.

'We have no more right to
consume happiness without
producing it than to consume
wealth without producing it.'
—*George Bernard Shaw*

'Only the development of
compassion and understanding
for others can bring us the
tranquility and happiness
we all seek.'
—*Dalai Lama XIV*

_____
_____
_____
_____
_____
_____
_____
_____
_____
_____
_____
_____

.Ruskin Bond.

.115.

.A Little Book of Happiness.

'I felt once more how simple and frugal a thing is happiness: a glass of wine, a roast chestnut, a wretched little brazier, the sound of the sea. Nothing else.'
—*Nikos Kazantzakis*

'Happiness. It comes on unexpectedly. And goes beyond, really, any early morning talk about it.'
—*Raymond Carver*

'God gave us our faces,'
said Granny, 'we give ourselves
our expressions.'

Granny again: 'Life may be
short, but a smile is only a
second's effort.'

The past is another country, someone has said, and it is good to go there on a visit once in a while. It is the small things I remember most vividly from my past. They come to me like pieces of cinema-coloured slides slipping across the screen of memory, bringing me solace, and sometimes a smile to my lips.

'The day returns and brings us the petty round of irritating concerns and duties. Help us play the man, help us to perform them with laughter and kind faces.'
—*Robert Louis Stevenson*

'The secret of happiness is not in doing what one likes, but in liking what one does.'
—*J.M. Barrie*

'My flute, M. Poirot, is my oldest
companion. When everything
else fails, music remains.'
—*Agatha Christie*

'My cat is selfish, smug and
ungrateful. Then she jumps onto
my lap and purrs, asking
to be loved, and I'm happy.'
—*Talula K.*

If you owe nothing, you are rich.
Money doesn't make
people happy.
But neither does poverty.
Just enough to be your own
person, and to lend a helping
hand—that much would be the
best, I suppose.

'A hot sun and a hot wind blowing; I go home and I am happy.'
—*An Italian proverb*

'The secret of happiness is to find a congenial monotony.'
—*V.S. Pritchett*

_____
_____
_____
_____
_____
_____
_____
_____
_____
_____
_____
_____
_____

⚜

.A Little Book of Happiness.

.Ruskin Bond.

.A Little Book of Happiness.

Even in Siberia there is happiness.

— Anton Chekhov

If you have the ability, or rather the gift, of being able to see beauty in small things, then life holds few terrors.

A cherry tree bowed down by the night's rain suddenly rights itself, flinging pellets of cool water in my face. This, too, is happiness.

.Ruskin Bond.

There is a flower I meet on my walk down to the bazaar these days. It has sprung out of a plastic mug in Mrs D's little balcony and is always nodding and dancing in the breeze. It is a happy flower, deserving of a happy, light name. I have named it Merry Heart, and sealed our friendship.

As I've grown older, I've stopped
fretting too much. I laugh
at myself more often; I don't
laugh at others. I live life
at my own pace.
And I am content.

🌿

'For some of us, happiness comes
while we sleep.'
—*A French proverb*

Slow down, there isn't always a train to catch. Make your walk as long and leisurely as possible, and you will find that the world you thought ugly is full of lovely little surprises.

For as long as I can remember, I have been the happiest taking a path—any old path will do—and following it until it leads me to a forest glade or village or stream or hilltop, or a face I long to see.

The adventure is not in arriving,
it's in the on-the-way experience.
It is not in the expected; it's
in the surprise. You are not
choosing what you shall see in
the world, but giving the world
an even chance to see you,
to get to know you and, perhaps,
show you just the things you
had longed to see but
could never find.

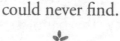

.Ruskin Bond.

Turn your attention to the sky,
look at the ever-changing cloud
patterns from your window.
There is no end to the shapes
made by the clouds, or to the
stories they set off in your head.
We don't have to circle the world
in order to find beauty
and fulfilment.

I remember the mouse who shared my room in London when I was seventeen and all on my own. He was a smart little mouse and sometimes he would speak to me—sharp little squeaks to remind me it was dinner time. The room was no longer as empty and lonely as when I had first moved in.

___
___
___
___
___
___
___
___
___
___
___
___

Each one of us is a mass of imperfections, and to recognize and live with our imperfections makes for an easier transit on life's journey.

'Those who bring sunshine into the lives of others cannot keep it from themselves.'
—*J.M. Barrie*

Children bring me joy. Sometimes I think small children are the only sacred things left on this earth. Children and flowers.

Help a stranger in distress, do it when there is nothing that requires you to do so, and you will find you are lighter, happier. And maybe one day a stranger will extend a hand when you stumble, and once again you will find happiness when you least expect it.

Sometimes, when all else fails, a sense of humour comes to the rescue. Laugh at yourself, laugh at fate, and soldier on.

By all means observe the conventions, but remember that it is only in personal independence that happiness is to be found. Stay free!

'Happiness…is not something that can be demanded from life, and if you are not happy you had better stop worrying about it and see what treasures you can pluck from your own brand of unhappiness.'
—*Robertson Davies*

'Make up your mind to be happy. Learn to find pleasure in simple things.'
—*Robert Louis Stevenson*

What if you failed yesterday?
Today is not yesterday.

❦

Nothing compares to the joy of hard-won success. Nothing is sweeter than victory at the end of many defeats.

❦

Even the most uninviting and unromantic places will surprise you with small miracles: moonlight on quiet alleys past midnight. Or the scent of quenched earth and fallen neem leaves after the first rains. Or the happy riot of the weekly bazaar.

He who has happy children
is greater than a king.
And he who spreads happiness
outside his home is greater still.

If one day you should lose all
your money, who knows—you
may become a happy yogi!
(If not, make peace with
your misery.)

Notes

.150.

.Ruskin Bond.

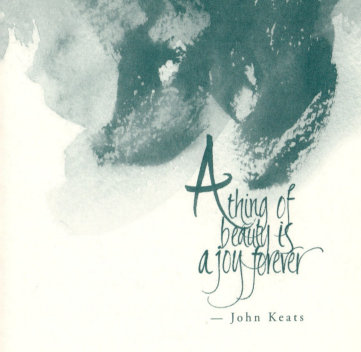

A thing of beauty is a joy forever

— John Keats

'Sometimes your joy is the source
of your smile, but sometimes
your smile can be the source
of your joy.'
—*Thich Nhat Hanh*

'Happiness is a how, not a what.
A talent, not an object.'
—*Hermann Hesse*

Life rarely plays by the rules.
Before you say, 'What did I do
to deserve such misfortune!'
think of all the times you found
happiness when you had done
little to deserve it.

Let us learn from the humble marigold. The rose may be the queen of flowers, and the jasmine the princess of fragrance, but the marigold holds its own through sheer sturdiness, colour and cheerfulness, brightening up winter days, often when there is little else in bloom.

'We must try to make the end of the journey better than the beginning, as long as we are journeying; but when we come to the end, we must be happy and content.'
—*Epicurus*

'The storm is over, there is sunlight in my heart.'
—*P.G. Wodehouse*

As a young man I planted a seed.
In old age I reap the rewards:
a wild cherry tree covered with
pale pink blossoms, and a little
yellow sunbird, emitting a
squeaky little song, flitting from
branch to branch.

'If you want a happy ending,
it just depends on where you
close the book!'
—*Orson Welles*

Dear reader, may you have the wisdom to be simple, and the humour to be happy.

Ruskin Bond is the author of numerous novellas, short-story collections and non-fiction books, many of them classics. Among them are *The Room on the Roof*, *A Flight of Pigeons*, *The Night Train at Deoli*, *Time Stops at Shamli*, *Landour Days*, *Rain in the Mountains*, *A Book of Simple Living* and *Friends in Wild Places*. He received the Sahitya Akademi Award in 1993, the Padma Shri in 1999 and the Padma Bhushan in 2014. He lives in Landour, Mussoorie, with his extended family.